New Mental Maths

5

Mridula Somayajulu

SCHOLARS HUB
NEW DELHI

CONTENTS

Date ____________

Exercise 1

1. How many 10 lakhs in 1 crore?

   ____

2. Write the period and place of the digit

   5 in 56324184 ______________________

   1 in 78516280 ______________________

   7 in 63729154 ______________________

3. Write the numeral for

   a. Fifteen crore, seven lakh, fifty six thousand, ten

   ____

   b. Three hundred sixty-three million, twelve thousand, two hundred

   ____

   c. One hundred eight million, four hundred one thousand, six

   ____

4. To which period 224 belongs in

   a. 224 128 295 ______________________

   b. 187 224 289 ______________________

   c. 352 187 224 ______________________

   d. 5 224 327 ______________________

Grade ________ Teacher's Signature ______________

Date ________

Exercise 2

1. Add the following:

a.
```
  1538609
  2075632
+ 5189089
---------

---------
```

b.
```
  5608351
  2739012
+ 1990650
---------

---------
```

c.
```
   698752
  1977016
+ 2038542
---------

---------
```

d.
```
  7089363
   238157
+ 8059342
---------

---------
```

2. How much

100 thousands = ____________ lakh

10 ten lakhs = ____________ ten lakh

1 lakh = ____________ thousand

10 lakhs = ____________ million

100 millions = ____________ crores

3. Write the numeral name of

a. 73 005 809 ____________

b. 315 201 008 ____________

c. 87 000 520 ____________

Grade ________ Teacher's Signature ________

Date ____________

Exercise 3

1. The difference between

   a. 95,34,075 and 1,50,41,655 ____________

   ____

   b. 2,16,05,480 and 92,75,075 ____________

   ____

2. The difference of two numbers is 97,82,651. The greater number is 1,79,86,941, the other number is ____________

   ____

3. 6,27,007 people appeared in All India Examination in year 2002. In year 2003 96,500 more people appeared in the same examination. The number of people appeared in the examination in year 2003 ____________

4. A fertilizer company produced 3,19,058 bags of fertilizers in year 2002. The production increased to 3,99,660 in the year 2003. The increase in production was ____________

   ____

5. Simplify : 93,74,650 – 52,28,540 + 19,14,590

   ____

Grade ________ Teacher's Signature ____________

Date ____________

Exercise 4

1. India produced 129580 tonnes of wheat in the year 1989-90, 1373256 tonnes of wheat in the year 90-91, 4489108 tonnes of wheat in the year 91-92. The total production of wheat from 1989 to 1992 is ____________ ____________.

2. In 1995 in India number of children, in the rural areas, going to primary school were 156789. In 1998, number of children, going to school, rose to 1448580. How many more children went to school in 1998 than in 1995? ____________ ____________.

3. The number of different brands of cars produced in India in the year 1999 were 2518350, in 2000 it was 750386, in 2001 it was 1561920. What is the total number of production in 2000 and 2001 ? ____________ ____________.

   In which year – 1999 or 2000 + 2001, the production of cars were more and by how much? ____________ ____________.

4. In a town there were 330359 children below 18 years of age. The number of girls were 72975 more than boys. The number of boys were 128692. The number of girls were ____________.

Grade ________ Teacher's Signature ____________

Date ____________

Exercise 5

1. Multiply and write the answer.

a.
```
  7 2 3 2
  x 5 0 9
---------
```

b.
```
  1 3 8 2 3
  x   1 7 5
-----------
```

2. a. Divide 740517372 by 252

b. Divide 53218638 by 99

3. Complete the following:

a.
```
      7 9 2 5 6
          x 2 3
---------------
    _ 7 7 _ 8
1 5 8 _ _ 2 x
---------------
_ _ _ _ _ _ 8
---------------
```

b.
```
          4 9
    -------------------
25 ) 1 2 3 3 0 7 5
     1 0 0
    -----
       2 3 3
       2 2 5
    -------
```

Grade ________ Teacher's Signature ____________

Date ____________

Exercise 6

1. Divide and write the quotient and the remainder.

   a. 8329183 ÷ 190

   b. 68932 ÷ 100

2. A factory produces 104545 pencils in a year. 35 pencils are packed in a box. The number of boxes required to pack all the pencils. ____

3. One room can accommodate 58 chairs. The number of chairs in 13 such rooms are ____________________.

4. In a plot of land same type of trees are planted equally in 218 rows. The number of trees are 4142 and the number of trees in each row are ____.

Grade ________ Teacher's Signature ____________

Date ____________

Exercise 7

1. ____________________ should be added to 95200 to get 15273600.

2. The product of 238941 and 150 is ______________ .

3. The remainder when dividend is 685426 and divisor is 127, ______________ .

4. 5600000 is ______________ more than 736250.

5. The quotient and remainder of 9473870 ÷ 100000 are ______________ and ______________ respectively.

6. The product of 196 and 10000 is ______________.

7. Complete the following:

```
     3 _ _ 8 9 3           4 6 _ 5 6 0
     2 5 6 _ _ 2             0 6 _ 2 9
 + _ 4 8 7 4 _           + 2 9 4 3 1
 -------------           -------------
     8 0 7 8 7 9         _ _ 9 3 _ 0
 -------------           -------------
```

8. 195 x ______________ = 19500000

9. Subtract 23956 from the sum of 156982 and 25856 ____ .

10. 45189 x 232 = 10583848

The division fact of above multiplicand is

____

Grade ________ Teacher's Signature ______________

Date ____________

Revision Ex. 1

1. Write in numerals with commas in appropriate places.

   a. Four crore sixty lakh twenty five thousand seven hundred fifteen. ____________

   b. Twenty-three lakh nineteen thousand forty.

   ____

2. The expenditure of a company in year 2002 was Rs 91,29,405. The expenditure increased by Rs 13,08,308 in the year 2003. The expenditure of the company in year 2003. ____________

3. Simplify 10,15,228 + 17,84,520 – 13,63,460

   ____

4. The cost of one bicycle is Rs 975. The cost of 225 such bicycles is ____________.

5. I divided 1,24,265 by a number. The quotient was 142 and the remainder 15. The divisor was ____________

   ____

6. 2,48,400 balls are equally packed in boxes. 144 balls fit in one box. The number of boxes for 2,48,400 balls are ____________.

Grade ________ Teacher's Signature ____________

Date ____________

Exercise 8

1. Find the HCF of 624, 780 and 988.

2. Find LCM of 840, 1085, 1470.

3. The greatest number that can divide 177 and 228 leaving remainders 2 and 3 respectively is ____________
____

4. The least length of a rope which can be made from pieces of lengths 18m, 24m and 12m is ____________
____

5. The smallest number which on division by 12, 15, 18 and 27 leaves remainder 3 in each case ____________
____

6. Find HCF of 84, 112

Grade ________ Teacher's Signature ____________

Date ____________

Exercise 9

1. The mixed fraction of $\frac{93}{7}$ is ______________.

2. The fraction of 23 is ______________ and reciprocal of 27 is ______________.

3. The improper fraction of $3\frac{7}{8}$ is ______________ and mixed fraction of $\frac{29}{3}$ is ______________.

4. The sum of 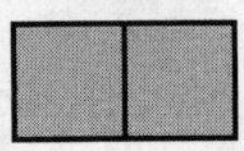 and 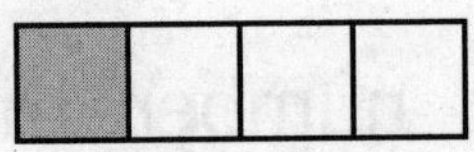 is ______________.

5. 4 times of $\frac{3}{2}$ is ______________.

6. $\frac{1}{2} = \frac{2}{4} = \frac{3}{\quad} = \frac{\quad}{8} = \frac{\quad}{\quad} = \frac{8}{\quad}$

7. The product of $\frac{5}{6}$ and $\frac{1}{2}$ is ______________.

8. The product of two fractions is $\frac{7}{8}$. One fraction is $\frac{1}{8}$, the other is ______________.

9. 12 half kgs of potatoes make __________ kg of potatoes.

10. In $\frac{6}{5}$, how many $\frac{1}{5}$ are there? ______________

Grade ________ Teacher's Signature ______________

Date ____________

Exercise 10

1. Write the fractions for the shaded portion.

a. 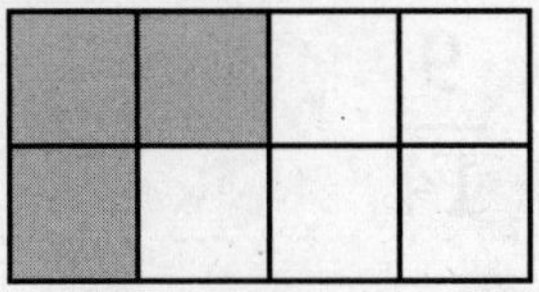 ________

b. 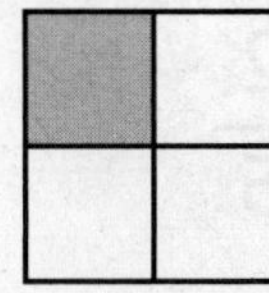 ________

c.  ________

d. 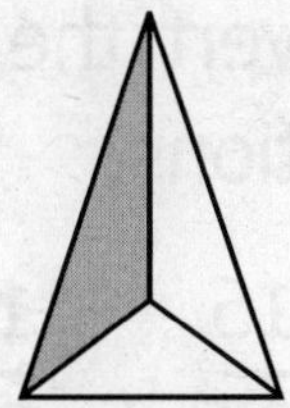 ________

2. Circle the equivalent fractions in each section.

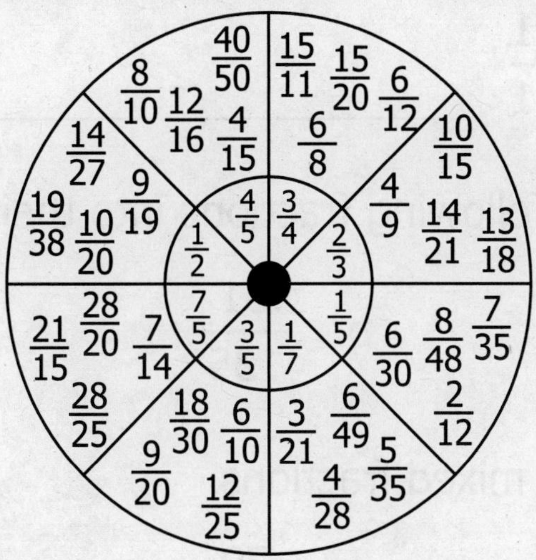

3. Make fraction equal to 1.

a. $\frac{5}{7} \times \quad = 1$

b. $\frac{3}{8} \times \quad = 1$

c. $\frac{11}{11} =$

d. $\frac{\quad}{13} \times \frac{\quad}{11} = 1$

Grade ________ Teacher's Signature ____________

Date ____________

Exercise 11

1. Change into equivalent fractions with numerator 18.

a. $\frac{2}{5}$ b. $\frac{6}{7}$ c. $\frac{9}{14}$ d. $\frac{3}{8}$

2. Convert the following pairs of unlike fractions into like fractions.

a. $\frac{15}{22}$, $\frac{17}{20}$ ____________________

b. $\frac{12}{35}$, $\frac{11}{21}$ ____________________

3. Reduce the following fractions into their lowest terms.

a. $\frac{160}{256}$ b. $\frac{81}{135}$ c. $\frac{102}{170}$

4. Convert into mixed fractions.

a. $\frac{67}{10}$ b. $\frac{79}{11}$ c. $\frac{46}{9}$

5. Convert into improper fractions

a. $15\frac{1}{3} =$ b. $6\frac{3}{4} =$

Grade ________ Teacher's Signature ____________

Date ____________

Exercise 12

1. Arrange the fraction in descending order.

   $\frac{4}{7}, \frac{19}{21}, \frac{11}{14}, \frac{2}{3}, \frac{25}{28}$ ____________________

2. Arrange the fractions in ascending order.

   $\frac{9}{10}, \frac{1}{2}, \frac{3}{5}, \frac{5}{8}, \frac{1}{4}$ ____________________

3. Subtract $8\frac{1}{2}$ from $11\frac{3}{4}$. ____________________

4. Simplify

   a. $15\frac{3}{14} + 6\frac{2}{7} - 10\frac{1}{2}$ ____________________

   b. $4\frac{2}{5} - 3\frac{1}{10} + 5\frac{1}{5}$ ____________________

5. A telephone pole is $7\frac{5}{6}$ metres tall. If $1\frac{2}{3}$ metres of the pole is below the ground, the pole above the ground is ____.

6. Prakash painted $\frac{3}{8}$ part of his room yellow, $\frac{1}{8}$ part blue and the rest green. The part he painted green was ____.

Grade ________ Teacher's Signature ____________

Date ____________

Exercise 13

1. The simplest form of

a. $\frac{9}{12} =$ | $\frac{1}{9}$, $\frac{12}{1}$, $\frac{3}{4}$, $\frac{4}{3}$

b. $\frac{25}{15} =$ | $\frac{5}{5}$, $\frac{5}{3}$, $\frac{1}{5}$, $\frac{3}{5}$

c. $\frac{27}{15} =$ | $\frac{3}{8}$, $\frac{7}{9}$, $\frac{9}{7}$, $\frac{3}{7}$

d. $\frac{18}{180} =$ | $\frac{10}{1}$, $\frac{1}{10}$, $\frac{1}{8}$, $\frac{1}{18}$

2. The mixed fractions are equal to improper fractions.

$2\frac{7}{5}$	$\frac{19}{2}$
$1\frac{8}{3}$	$\frac{93}{7}$
$9\frac{1}{2}$	$\frac{17}{5}$
$11\frac{3}{5}$	$\frac{61}{5}$
$13\frac{2}{7}$	$\frac{11}{3}$
$12\frac{1}{5}$	$\frac{58}{5}$

Grade ________ Teacher's Signature ____________

Date ____________

Exercise 14

1. Find the product of

 a. $\frac{2}{7}$ and $\frac{3}{10}$ = ____________________

 b. $1\frac{2}{7}$ and $7\frac{1}{5}$ = ____________________

 c. $\frac{3}{8}$ and $3\frac{2}{7}$ = ____________________

2. Make 4 equivalent fractions of

 a. $\frac{3}{7}$ ____________________

 b. $\frac{5}{9}$ ____________________

 c. $\frac{11}{13}$ ____________________

 d. $\frac{15}{7}$ ____________________

3. Multiply

 a. $\left[2\frac{1}{4} \times 5\frac{1}{3}\right] \times 4\frac{1}{2}$

 ____

Grade __________ Teacher's Signature ____________

Date ____________

Exercise 15

1. Fit the jig-saw with the correct answer.

$\frac{7}{5} \times 5$

$\frac{11}{17} \times \frac{17}{11}$

$\frac{125}{125} \times 5$

$\frac{18}{5} \times \frac{15}{9}$

5

7

6

1

2. Represent the following

a. $\frac{3}{4}$ of 20

b. $\frac{2}{3}$ of 12

c. $\frac{5}{7}$ of 14

Grade ________ Teacher's Signature ____________

Date ____________

Exercise 16

1. Find the product.

a. $\frac{8}{6} \times \frac{6}{8} \times 1 =$ ____________

b. $1 \times \frac{7}{7} \times \frac{9}{9} =$ ____________

c. $\frac{13}{15} \times \frac{15}{13} =$ ____________

d. $1\frac{7}{5} \times 2\frac{3}{5} \times 0 =$ ____________

2. Say whether ✓ or ✗.

a. $\frac{1}{7} \times 7 = 0$ ______

b. $1\frac{5}{7} \times 3\frac{5}{3} = \frac{12}{7} \times \frac{14}{3} = 8$ ______

c. $\frac{100}{1000} \times 10 = 1$ ______

d. $\frac{150}{300} \times \frac{100}{100} = 1$ ______

Then write the correct answers for the wrong ones.

Grade ________ Teacher's Signature ____________

Date ________

Exercise 17

1. Make the following fractions equal to 1.

a. $\frac{15}{18} =$ b. $1\frac{7}{9} =$

c. $3\frac{2}{11} =$ d. $\frac{22}{55} =$

2. Fill in the blanks.

a. $\frac{1}{3} \div 5 = \frac{1}{3} \times$ ______ = ______

b. $\frac{2}{7} \div \frac{11}{5} =$ ______ = ______

c. $\frac{19}{5} \div \frac{19}{5} =$ ______ = ______

d. $\frac{29}{11} \div$ ______ = ______ = 1

3. Write > or < in the following.

a. $\frac{3}{5} \square \frac{3}{7}$ b. $\frac{15}{16} \square \frac{23}{24}$

c. $\frac{1}{5} \square \frac{2}{9}$ d. $\frac{3}{5} \square \frac{9}{20}$

Grade ________ Teacher's Signature ________

Date ________

Exercise 18

1. Divide and write the quotient.

a. $30 \div \frac{3}{4} =$ ____________________

b. $75 \div \frac{5}{7} =$ ____________________

c. $100 \div \frac{10}{1} =$ ____________________

d. $72 \div \frac{12}{7} =$ ____________________

2. Put ✓ or ✗ against each statement.

a. The multiplicative inverse of 0 is 0.

b. When a non-zero fractional number is divided by itself, the quotient is 1.

c. The product of a fractional number and its multiplicative inverse is 0.

d. $\frac{2}{3} \div \frac{1}{5}$ means $\frac{2}{3}$ of $\frac{1}{5}$.

e. There is only one number which is multiplicative inverse of itself.

Grade ________ Teacher's Signature ________

Date ____________

Revision Ex. 2

1. Simplify

a. $8\frac{1}{4} + 5\frac{1}{3} - 9\frac{1}{2}$ b. $\frac{11}{5} + \frac{4}{5} - \frac{2}{3}$

________________ ________________

________________ ________________

2. The multiplicative inverse of

a. 25 b. $8\frac{1}{7}$ c. $\frac{23}{15}$

3. There are 750 seats in an auditorium. $\frac{13}{15}$ of the seats were filled for a programme. The number of people attended the programme were ________________.

4. The product of two numbers is $25\frac{5}{6}$. If one of the numbers is $8\frac{1}{3}$, the other number is ____________.

5. Rani bought $9\frac{1}{2}$ metres of a cloth at the rate of Rs 18 per metre. Rani spent ________________________.

6. Divide

a. $50 \div 8\frac{1}{3}$ b. $52 \div 6\frac{1}{2}$

Grade ________ Teacher's Signature ____________

Date ____________

Exercise 19

1. Draw figures and show the following fractions.

   a. $\frac{1}{4}$ of 1

   b. $\frac{2}{3}$ of 1

2. Solve the following.

   a. A family consumes $2\frac{1}{2}$ litres of milk daily. The amount of milk consumed in the month of September was ______________________.

   b. Anju bought 8 metres of cloth. She made pieces each of $\frac{1}{2}$ metre. The number of pieces she made were ______________________.

   c. In a village $\frac{1}{2}$ the population is of men. Out of this $\frac{2}{3}$ of the men are illiterate. The fraction of illiterate men are ______________________.

   d. A football team won 3 matches more than it lost. It won $\frac{2}{5}$ of its matches, the total number of matches played ______________________.

Grade ________ Teacher's Signature ____________

Date ____________

Exercise 20

1. Write the expanded form of

a. 100.007 ______________________

b. 19.853 ______________________

c. 358.005 ______________________

d. 808.008 ______________________

2. How many

a. 10 tenths = ________ one

b. 100 thousandths = ________ tenths

c. 20 tenths = ________ ones

d. 600 tenths = ________ tens

e. 200 hundredths = ________ ones

3. Shade only that part of the train which has the correct answer

a.

41.85=	40+10 +.8+.5	40+1+ .8+.05	4+10+ 8.0+5.0	41+.8 +.5

b.

5.707=	50+.7 +.7	5+.07 +.07	50+.7 +.007	5+.7 +.007

Grade ________ Teacher's Signature ______________

Date ____________

Exercise 21

1. Expand into ones and tenths.

   a. 50 tenths = ____________ + ____________

   b. 72 tenths = ____________ + ____________

   c. 19 tenths = ____________ + ____________

2. Expand into tenths and hundreths.

   a. 25 hundredths = ____________ + ____________

   b. 81 hundredths = ____________ + ____________

   c. 30 hundredths = ____________ + ____________

   d. 16 hundredths = ____________ + ____________

3. Convert the following into ones.

   a. 50 tenths = ____________

   b. 500 tenths = ____________

   c. 150 tenths = ____________

   d. 70 tenths = ____________

   e. 90 tenths = ____________

Grade ________ Teacher's Signature ____________

Date ______________

Exercise 22

1. Match the decimal to its correct fraction.

Decimal	Fraction
.77	$\frac{5108}{100}$
51.08	$\frac{1751}{1000}$
112.16	$\frac{415}{1000}$
1.751	$\frac{11216}{100}$
.415	$\frac{77}{100}$

2. Who is what ?

Unlike decimals

Like decimals

- 11.18
- 11.108
- 1.15
- 15.671

- 1.17
- 2.15
- 1.19
- 215.25

- .20
- .02
- .002

- 6.05
- 6.105
- 7.2
- 70.18

- 2.189
- 15.156
- 2.205
- 191.180

Grade ________ Teacher's Signature ______________

Date ____________

Exercise 23

1. Change unlike decimals to like decimals.

   a. 14.89, 29.4, 9.3 ____________

   b. 115.105, 25.7, 18.15 ____________

   c. .9, 1.28, .5, 17.89 ____________

2. Shade the following to show the fraction.

$\frac{5}{10}$

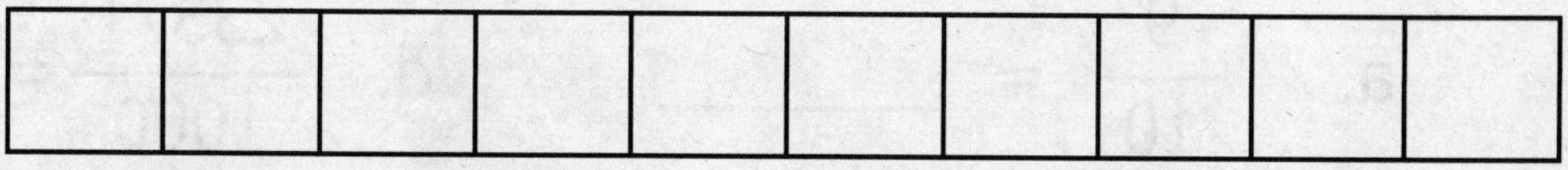

$\frac{5}{12}$

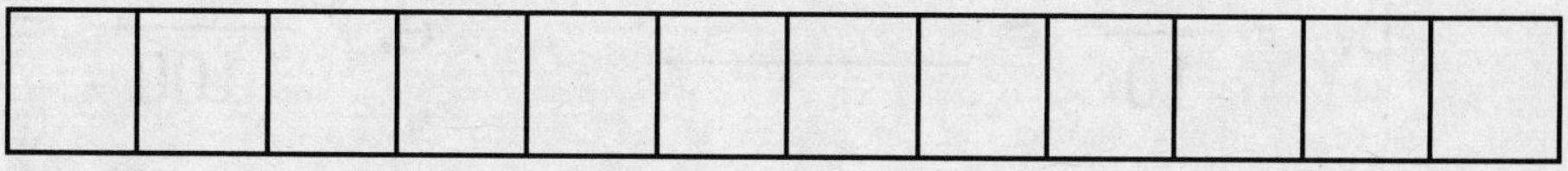

$\frac{1}{8}$

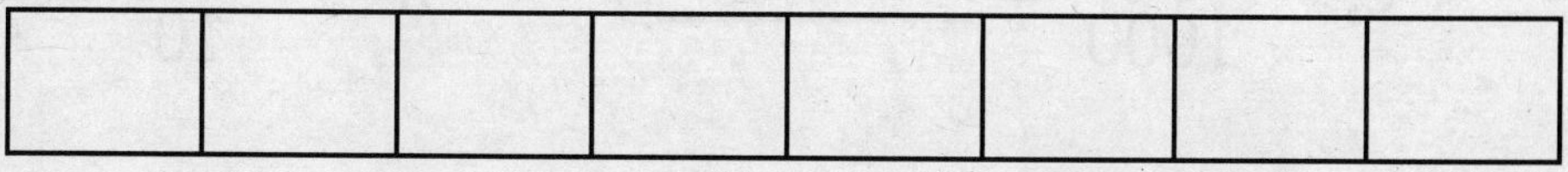

$\frac{7}{15}$

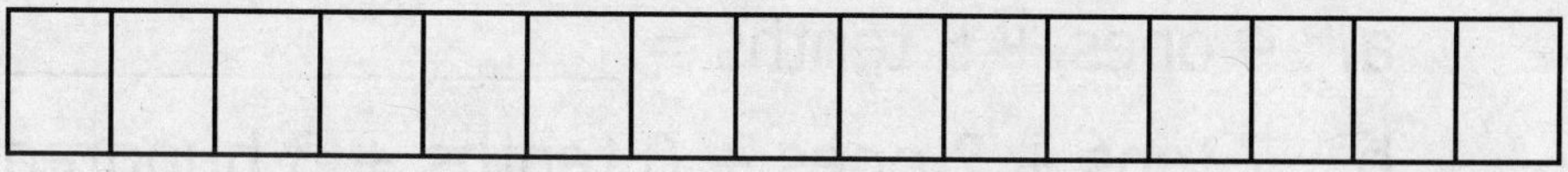

$\frac{3}{20}$

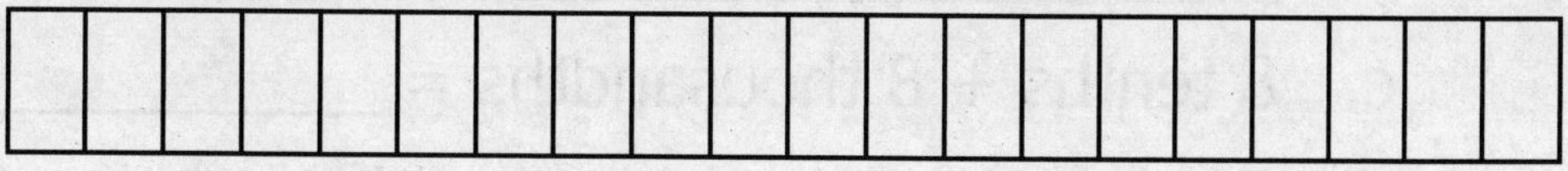

Grade ________ Teacher's Signature ____________

Date ____________

Exercise 24

1. Write > or < in the ☐.

a. .49 ☐ .419
b. .99 ☐ .89
c. .55 ☐ .15
d. .335 ☐ .430
e. .101 ☐ .11
f. .150 ☐ .1

2. Write the decimal of the following fractions.

a. $\frac{9}{10}$ = ____________
b. $\frac{41}{10}$ = ____________
c. $\frac{719}{1000}$ = ____________
d. $\frac{23571}{1000}$ = ____________
e. $\frac{199}{100}$ = ____________
f. $\frac{283}{10}$ = ____________

3. Write the decimals of

a. 4 ones + 5 tenths = ____________
b. 7 tens + 2 ones + 6 tenths + 3 hundredths =
____
c. 8 tenths + 8 thousandths = ____________
d. zero tenths + zero hundredths + 1 thousandths =
____

Grade ________ Teacher's Signature ____________

Date ____________

Exercise 25

1. Represent the following decimals in the place value chart.

a. 73.26 b. 591.08 c. 1024.875 d. 69107.504

2. Write the expanded form in numerals.

a. 67.2 = ____________________

b. 932.01 = ____________________

c. 30704.003 = ____________________

3. Write the standard form of

a. $10000 + 400 + 30 + \frac{2}{10} + \frac{6}{100} + \frac{7}{1000}$

b. $6000 + 100 + 20 + 8 + \frac{7}{10} + \frac{4}{100} + \frac{3}{1000}$

4. Convert into decimals.

a. $3\frac{1}{8} =$

b. $\frac{24}{15} =$

Grade ________ Teacher's Signature ____________

Date ______________

Exercise 26

1. Make it equal to ...

   a. 7 tenths + 3 thousandths = ______ tenths + ______ hundredths + ______ thousandths

   b. 4 hundredths + 5 thousandths = 6 hundredths + ______ thousandths

   c. 5 ones + 7 tenths = 4 ones + ______ tenths

   d. 3 tenths + 2 hundredths + 5 thousandths = 2 tenths + ____ hundredths + ____ thousandths

   e. 6 tenths + 2 thousandths = ______ tenths + ______ hundredths + ______ thousandths

2. Change the decimals into like decimals and add.

   a. 1.18, 5.2, .7 ______________________________

   ____

   b. .56, .651, 8.23 ______________________________

   ____

   c. 9.2, 11.05, 7.189 ______________________________

   ____

Grade ________ Teacher's Signature ______________

Date ____________

Exercise 27

1. Join the decimals whose answers are the same.

19.51 + 1.07	42.190 – 22.955
5.365 + 3.002 + .052	107.440 – 25.774
1.05 + 12.385 + 5.8	12.25 + 8.33
76.2 + 2.76 + 2.706	41.23 + 405.09 + 8.582
45.2 + 4.502 + 405.2	11.205 – 2.786

2. Who spent more money ?

Anita

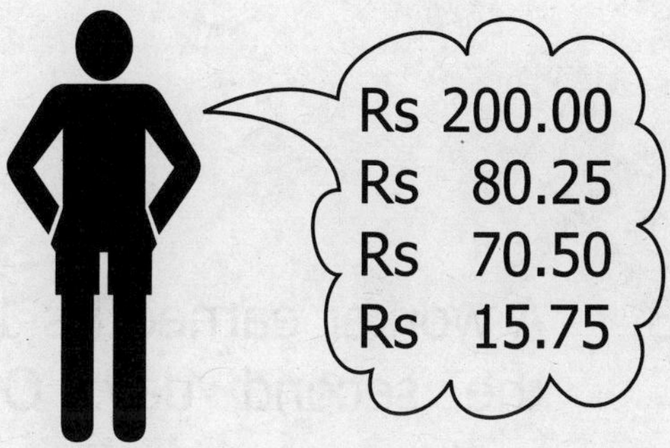

Suraj

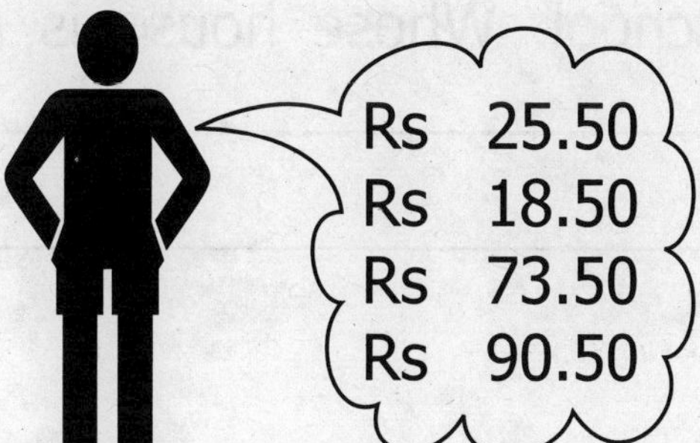

Hari

Ankita

Grade ________ Teacher's Signature ____________

Date ____________

Exercise 28

1. Arrange in columns and add.

   a. 1.7, 100.18, 0.982 b. 29.58, 285.9, 2.598

2. Arrange in columns and subtract.

   a. 138.7 – 59.8 b. 35.8 – 16.757

3. A worker earned Rs 195.25 on a day and Rs 155.00 on the second day. On which day he earned more __________. How much more did he earn ? __________

4. Vineet's house is 12.5 km from school and Vinay's house is 9.5 km from school. Whose house is more distant from school ? ______________________

   ____

   By how many kilometres ?

   ____

Grade ________ Teacher's Signature ______________

Date ____________

Exercise 29

1. Subtract 15.09 from the sum of 109.2 and 13.12.

   ____

2. What should be added to 18.215 to get 37.30 ?

   ____

3. Harinder ran a race in 13.15 seconds and Tapas ran the same distance for 13.012 seconds. Who ran faster and by how much ?

   ____

4. A cloth merchant had 55 m of a cloth. Anjali bought 15.25 m of cloth. Sujatha bought 20.75 m and Neera bought 12.50 m of the same cloth. The length of cloth left with the shopkeeper ______________________

   ____.

5. The difference between the height of Rohit 155.15 m and Ravi 152.085 m is ______________________.

6. The weight of box A is 65.152 kg more than box . which weighs 31.250 kg. The weight of box A is

   ____.

Grade ________ Teacher's Signature ____________

Date ____________

Exercise 30

1. Multiply the following.

   a. 0.1 x 5 =

   b. 0.7 x 3 =

   c. 2.7 x 4 =

   d. 5.56 x 6 =

2. Find the product.

   a. 165.18 x 23   b. 6.356 x 115

3. Fill in the blanks.

   a. 8.3 x 5 = 8.3 + 8.3 + ____________

   b. $\frac{19}{10}$ = ____________

   c. 16.50 + 16.50 + 16.50 = 16.50 x ____________

   d. 55.279 – 8.320 + 12.1 = ____________

Grade ________   Teacher's Signature ____________

Date ____________

Exercise 31

1. Put decimal in the correct place in the answer.

   a. 13.75 x 7.3 = 100375

   b. 6.01 x 9.32 = 560132

   c. .56 x .83 = 4648

   d. .37 x .01 = 37

2. Divide and write the quotient.

   a. .24 ÷ 6 = ________

   b. .088 ÷ 8 = ________

   c. 0.625 ÷ 5 = ________

   d. .192 ÷ 12 = ________

   e. .017 ÷ 17 = ________

   f. 3.12 ÷ 8 = ________

3. If 1275 ÷ 15 = 85, find the quotient in each of the following.

   a. 1.275 ÷ 15 = _______

   b. 12.75 ÷ 15 = _______

   c. .1275 ÷ 15 = _______

   d. 127.5 ÷ 15 = _______

4. Multiply

   a. 4.123 x 100 = ________________

   b. 99.99 x 100 = ________________

   c. .635 x 10 = ________________

   d. 989.05 x 1000 = ________________

Grade ________ Teacher's Signature ____________

Date ______________

Exercise 32

1. Divide and find the quotient.

a. 84 ÷ 3.5 = ______

b. 29 ÷ 0.232 = ______

c. 133 ÷ 95 = ______

d. 0.284 ÷ 7.1 = ______

e. 34.72 ÷ 2.17 = ______

f. 26 ÷ 104 = ______

2. Answer the following.

a. 543 kilograms of sugar is filled equally in 12 bags. The amount of sugar in each bag ______________.

b. The cost of a notebook is Rs 11.50 and that of a pen is Rs 9.50. Priti bought 3 notebooks and 5 pens. The money spent on notebooks and pens is ______________________________.

c. One shirt is made of 1.8 metres of cloth. The number of shirts made by 45 metres long cloth is ______________________________.

d. A bag contains 74.650 kg of wheat. The amount of wheat in 15 such bags are ______________.

Grade ________ Teacher's Signature ______________

Date ______________

Exercise 33

1. If 76 x 48 = 3648, the product of the following.

a. 7.6 x 48 = ________

b. 76 x 4.8 = ________

c. 7.6 x 4.8 = ________

d. .76 x 48 = ________

e. .76 x .48 = ________

f. .76 x 4.8 = ________

2. Divide

a. 28 by 0.07

b. 36 by 32

c. $0.621 \div 0.27$

d. $100 \div 32$

3. Find the quotient.

a. $80.4 \div 4000$

b. $950.4 \div 9000$

Grade ________ Teacher's Signature ______________

Date ____________

Exercise 34

1 litre = 1000 ml	1m = 100 cm
1 kg = 1000 grams	1 rupee = 100 paise

1. How much in rupees?

   1250 paise = __________ rupees

   12 rupees 75 paise = __________ rupees

2. Express in metres and centimetres.

   a. 5.65 m = __________

   b. .60 m = __________

   c. 12.85 m = __________

   d. 17.08 m = __________

3. How many millilitres?

   a. 1.75 l = __________

   b. 9.25 l = __________

4. How many grams?

   a. 0.035 kg = __________

   b. 6.500 kg = __________

5. How many kilograms?

   a. 800 g = __________

   b. 6 kg 300 g = __________

6. Convert into litres.

   a. 225 ml = __________

   b. 750 ml = __________

Grade ________ Teacher's Signature ____________

Date ____________

Exercise 35

1. Simplify and write.

a. $14 - 7 + 25 \div 5 \times 2$

b. $50 + 10 - 18 \div 2 \times 5$

c. $\frac{19}{4} + \frac{51}{4} \div \frac{17}{3} - \frac{7}{4}$

d. $5\frac{1}{4} + 3\frac{1}{9} \div 2\frac{1}{3} - 6\frac{1}{3}$

2. Simplify

a. $3.5 - 0.5 + 5 \times 1.5$

b. $3 \times 1 - \frac{1}{3} \times \frac{1}{3} \div 3$

c. $9\frac{1}{6} + 8\frac{1}{3} - 11\frac{3}{4}$

d. $12\frac{2}{9} \div 5\frac{1}{9}$

e. $6.2 \times 1.5 - 2 \times 3.1 + 0.9$

f. $3.25 \div 0.25 + 10.5$

g. $9\frac{2}{8} - 8\frac{3}{4} + 4\frac{3}{16}$

h. $7\frac{2}{8} \div 5\frac{4}{5}$

Grade ________ Teacher's Signature ____________

Date ____________

Exercise 36

1. The length of a ribbon is 65 cm. Aarti bought 7 such ribbons. The total length of the ribbon is ____.

2. 4.5 litres of milk is to be filled in 250 ml bottles. The bottles needed to fill the whole milk are ____.

3. Convert
   a. 32 g into cg ______________
   b. 2890 mg into g ______________
   c. 850 cl into litres ______________
   d. 7500 l into kl ______________
   e. 640 l into hl ______________
   f. 375 m into hm ______________
   g. 94 m into dam ______________
   h. 804 mm into m ______________
   i. 4250 m into km ______________
   j. 23 mm into cm ______________
   k. 30 hm into m ______________

1 g = 100 cg	1 cl = $\frac{1}{100}$ l	100 m = 1 hm
1 mg = $\frac{1}{1000}$ g	1 l = $\frac{1}{1000}$ kl	1 dam = 1 m

Grade ________ Teacher's Signature ______________

Date ____________

Revision Ex. 3

1. Divide

19.2 ÷ 10 = ________

19.2 ÷ 1000 = ________

19.2 ÷ 100 = ________

2. Fill in the blanks.

a. 46.9 x ____ = 0

b. ____ x 10.6 = ____ x 8.3

c. 97.8 x 0 = ____

g. 0.8 x 5.1 = ____ x 0.8

e. ____ x 1 = 23.64

f. ____ x 1 = 50.5

d. 9.17 x 1 = ____

h. 8.05 x ____ = 8.05

3. What is to be added to 17.348 to get 35 ?

____

4. Add 106.75, 96.103, 8.2

____

5. What is to be subtracted from 81.14 to get 43.725?

____

6. Divide

a. 50.05 ÷ 7

b. 1.068 ÷ 12

Grade ________ Teacher's Signature ____________

Date ____________

Exercise 37

1. While rounding to nearest thousand which numbers could be rounded to

   a. 8000 ____________ b. 35000 ____________

2. Round off to nearest hundred

   a. 1090 ____________ b. 4561 ____________

3. Round off to nearest ten thousand

   a. 72514 ____________ b. 60200 ____________

4. Round off to nearest lakh

   a. 950126 ____________ b. 570096 ____________

5. Round off to nearest ten.

   a. 816 ____________ c. 75 ____________

   b. 2415 ____________ d. 1005 ____________

6. Write the following in Roman numerals.

   a. 980 = ____________________

   b. 169 = ____________________

   c. 84 = ____________________

7. Write Hindu Arabic numeral of

   a. DCCLXIX ____________________

   b. CCCXXV ____________________

Grade ________ Teacher's Signature ____________

Date ____________

Exercise 38

1. Rounding off.

   a. 93 is rounded to ________

   b. 6190 is rounded to ________

   c. 3240 is rounded to ________

   d. 756 is rounded to ________

   e. 414 is rounded to ________

   f. 1717 is rounded to ________

2. Round off to ...

a.	nearest lakh	1542364	____________
b.	nearest crore	84030110	____________
c.	nearest thousand	60761	____________
d.	nearest ten thousand	999910	____________

3. Write in Roman numerals.

   a. Eight two ________

   b. Seventy eight ________

   c. Ninety nine ________

   d. Fifty four ________

4. Change into Hindu-Arabic numerals.

   a. LXXIX ________

   b. C ________

   c. XLV ________

   d. CMXX ________

   e. CML ________

   f. DCCCX ________

Grade ________ Teacher's Signature ____________

Date ____________

Exercise 39

1. Write as percentages.

   a. Seventy hundredths ____________

   b. Twenty nine hundredths ____________

2. Express as percentages.

   a. 2.7 ____________

   c. 0.09 ____________

   b. 0.55 ____________

   d. 0.5 ____________

3. Convert into decimals.

   a. 19.4% ____________

   c. 17.5% ____________

   b. 340% ____________

   d. 97% ____________

4. Which is equivalent to 8%?

   0.08, .8, .008, 8

5. Express as percentage of a rupee.

   a. 67 paise ____________

   b. 7 paise ____________

Grade ________ Teacher's Signature ____________

Date ____________

Exercise 40

1. It's percentage in a litre is

   a. 85 ml ____________ c. 880 ml ____________

   b. 810 ml ____________ d. 500 ml ____________

2. Which is more?

   a. 20% of 500 or 20% of 200 ____________

   b. 15% of 800 or 25% of 700 ____________

   c. 10% of 650 or 15% of 500 ____________

3. Find the value of

   a. $10\frac{1}{4}$ % of Rs 800 ____________

   b. $9\frac{1}{2}$ % of Rs 1200 ____________

   c. 18% of 250 g ____________

4. In a test comprising of 30 questions of equal marks, Surbhi scored 70% marks. The number of questions answered correctly were ____________.

5. Out of 40 students, 80% of them went for excursion. The number of students who did not go for the trip were ____.

Grade ________ Teacher's Signature ____________

Date ____________

Exercise 41

1. Change the following.
   a. 4015 cm into m ____________
   b. 6200 mm into m ____________
   c. 6.5 km into m ____________
   d. 375 m into hm ____________
2. Convert
   a. 75 cg into dg ____________
   b. 2890 mg into g ____________
   c. 5.4 g into mg ____________
   d. 750 g into hg ____________
   e. 2890 mg into g ____________
   f. 500 dam into km ____________
   g. 40 mm into cm ____________
   h. 804 mm into m ____________

1 dam = 10 m	1 kg = 1000 g	1 ml = $\frac{1}{1000}$ l
1 hm = 100 m	1 hg = 100 g	1 l = $\frac{1}{1000}$ kl
1 km = 1000 m	1 dag = 10 g	1 l = $\frac{1}{100}$ hl
1 mm = $\frac{1}{1000}$ m	1 mg = $\frac{1}{1000}$ g	
1 dm = $\frac{1}{10}$ m	1 dg = 100 mg	
1 m = 100 cm		

Grade ________ Teacher's Signature ____________

Date ______________

Exercise 42

1. Convert

    a. 7500 l into kl ______________

    b. 640 l into hl ______________

    c. 53 l into ml ______________

    d. 610 ml into l ______________

2. Answer the following.

    a. Suman bought 2l 250ml of milk. She used 650 ml of milk to make sweets. The amount of milk left was ______________________________.

    b. A train travels 437.5 km in 7 hours. The number of km it travelled in one hour ______________.

    c. 1627.5 kg of onions are packed equally in 35 bags. Onions in each bag ______________.

    d. 4.5 litres of milk is to be filled in 250 ml bottles. The number of bottles needed to fill the whole milk are ______________________________.

Grade ________ Teacher's Signature ______________

Date ____________

Exercise 43

1. Convert

   a. $10\frac{1}{2}$ days into hours ____________

   b. 6 days 6 hours into hours ____________

   c. $3\frac{3}{4}$ hours into minutes ____________

   d. $3\frac{1}{2}$ hours into seconds ____________

   e. 465 seconds into minutes ____________

   f. 21600 seconds into hours ____________

   g. 288 hours into days ____________

   h. 2 hours into seconds ____________

   i. 25200 seconds into hours ____________

2. The duration of time period from 10.30 a.m. to 3 p.m. is ____________.

3. The sum of 6 hours 5 minutes and 4 hours 30 minutes is ____________.

4. The duration from 15 January to 20 March of the same year is ____________.

5. A cricket match started at 9.30 a.m. and ended at 5 p.m. The duration of match was ____________.

Grade ________ Teacher's Signature ____________

Date ____________

Revision Ex. 4

1. Round off to

   a. nearest thousand — 1398 ____________

   b. nearest lakh — 4,53,850 ____________

2. Find the following.

   a. 40% of 140 ____________

   b. 35% of 20 kg ____________

3. Express in lowest terms.

   a. 98%   b. $6\frac{1}{4}\%$ c. 150%   d. $16\frac{2}{3}\%$

4. Express as a percentage of a metre.

   a. 64 cm   b. 100 cm   c. 82 cm

   ____________   ____________   ____________

5. a. 1000 grams = _______ % of a kilogram

   b. 250 grams = _______ % of a kilogram

   c. 10 ml = _______ % of a litre

   d. 2 ml = _______ % of a litre

   e. 25 cm = _______ % of a metre

   f. 90 cm = _______ % of a metre

   g. 75 paise = _______ % of a rupee

Grade ________   Teacher's Signature ____________

Date ____________

Exercise 44

1. Answer the following.

   a. The cost of 15 shirts of the same quality is Rs 8250. The cost of each shirt is ______________.

   b. The cost of 3 dozen bananas is Rs 45. The cost of 1 dozen is ______________ and the cost of 1 banana is ______________.

   c. The cost of 3 dozen eggs is Rs 75. The cost of 1 dozen eggs is ______________.

   d. The cost of 15 toffees is Rs 12. The cost of 7 toffees is ______________.

   e. The cost of a box of 18 kg of apples is Rs 396. The cost of 10 kg of apples is ______________.

   f. Sonali sold her refrigerator for Rs 15650 at a profit of Rs 875. The cost price of the refrigerator ______________.

   g. The cost price of a scooter is Rs 19280. It is sold at a loss of Rs 3500. The selling price is ____________.

   h. Anil bought two radio sets for Rs 1630. He sold one of them for Rs 750 and the other for Rs 850. His profit or loss on the sale of two radio sets is ______________.

Grade ________ Teacher's Signature ______________

Date ____________

Exercise 45

1. Convert into Fahrenheit.

   a. 36°C ____________ c. 42°C ____________

   b. 75°C ____________ d. 17°C ____________

2. Convert into degree Celsius.

   a. 43°F ____________ c. 122°F ____________

   b. 50°F ____________ d. 149°F ____________

3. The duration from

   a. March 5, 2000 to January 15, 2002.

   ____

   b. February 5 to July 25 of the year 2003.

   ____

4. The freezing point of water on the Fahrenheit scale is ______________________________________.

5. The boiling point of water on the Celsius scale is ______________________________________.

6. The body temperature of a person in normal conditions is ____________ °F.

Grade ________ Teacher's Signature ________________

Date ____________

Exercise 46

1. Name the angles.

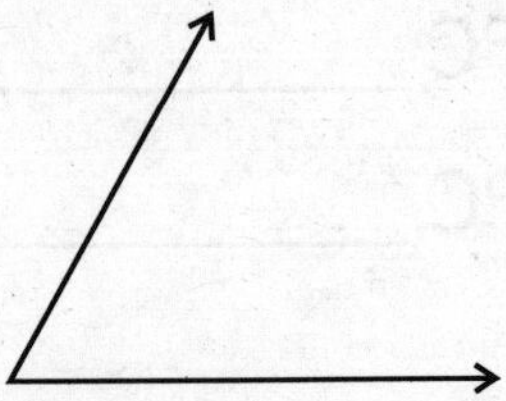  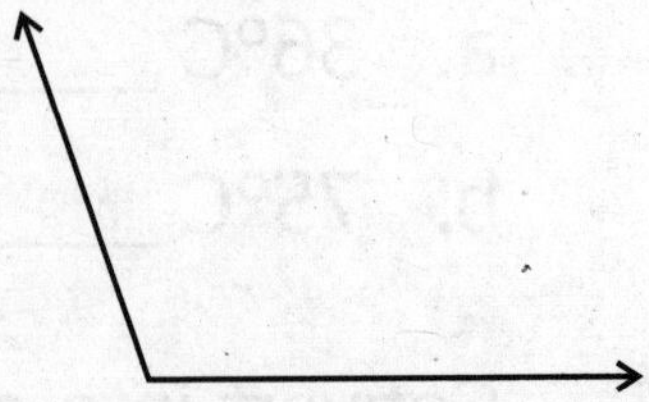

____________ ____________ ____________

2. Draw the following angles.

a. 25° b. 130° c. 95°

3. Answer the following.

a. An angle whose measure is 180° is called a ____________ angle.

b. An angle has one __________ and two __________.

c. An obtuse angle is always ___________ 90° but ___________ 180°.

d. A line has ___________ end points.

e. A plane cannot be ___________ on a paper.

f. A ray has ___________ end point.

g. A line segment has ___________ end points.

Grade ________ Teacher's Signature ______________

Date ____________

Exercise 47

1. Name all the three angles of this triangle.

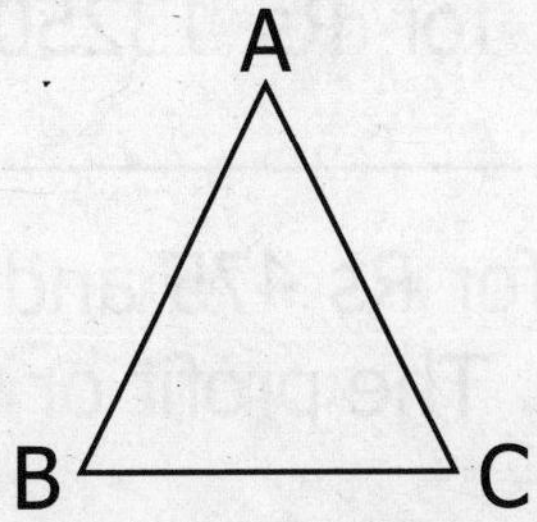

____

____

____

2. Find the third angle.

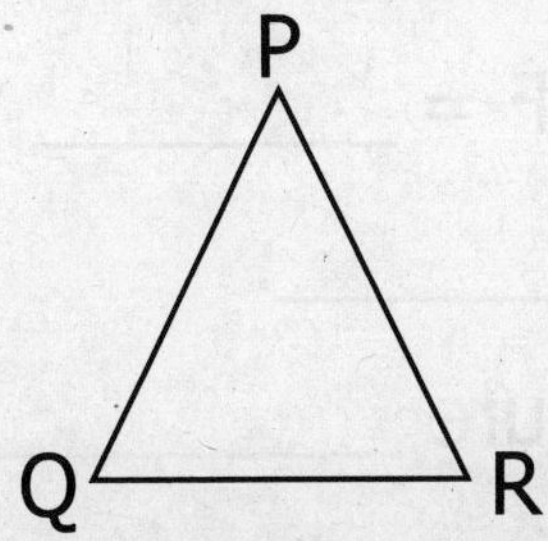

$\angle PQR = 60°$

$\angle QPR = 50°$

____

3. Say 'Yes' or 'No' in the following.
   a. Can triangle be drawn with 50°, 40°, 100°? ______
   b. Can triangle be drawn with 3cm, 2cm, 6cm? ______
   c. Can triangle be drawn with 7cm, 5cm, 8cm? ______
   d. Can triangle be drawn with 90°, 50°, 40°? ______
   e. Can triangle be drawn with 4cm, 6cm, 5cm? ______

4. A triangle ΔEFG has all the three angles equal. The measure of each angle is ___________.

5. A triangle is made up of ___________ points.

6. A triangle is made up of ____ sides, ____ vertices and ____ angles.

Grade ________ Teacher's Signature ________________

Date ____________

Revision Ex. 5

1. A dealer purchases washing machines each for Rs 10600. He sells each machine for Rs 13250. The gain is ______________________________.

2. Arjun bought two wall clocks. One for Rs 475 and other for Rs 385. He sold both for Rs 950. The profit or loss is ______________________________.

3. Convert

   75°C = __________ °F 113°F = __________ °C

4. a. A straight angle measures ____________.

   b. Three angles of a triangle measure ____________.

   c. A triangle is made up of ____________ line segments.

   d. The measure of a right angle is ____________.

   e. A full circle is ____________ degrees in measure.

5. Draw angles of measure

   a. 60° b. 145° c. 180°

Grade ________ Teacher's Signature ______________

Date ____________

Exercise 48

1. Find out the radii.

   Diameter is 14cm ____________

   Diameter is 10cm ____________

2. The radius is 3cm, the diameter is ________.

3. The length of one complete round along a circle is called the ________ of the circle.

4. A circle is drawn using a ________.

5. A line segment joining any two points of a circle is called a ________ of a circle.

6. In a circle draw a

   diameter AB

   chord PQ

   radius OB

7. Half of circle is called a ____________.

8. The diameter of a circle is 12cm. Its circumference approximately equals to ________.

9. Draw a circle of radius 4cm. With the same centre another circle of radius 3cm. What are these circles called? ____________

Grade ________ Teacher's Signature ____________

Date ____________

Exercise 49

1. Find the area of the following figures.

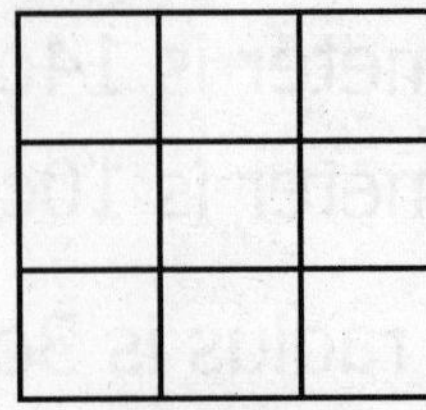

____________ ____________

2. a. The perimetre of a square whose sides are of 7.5cm each is ______________________________.

   b. The area of a square whose each side is of 7.5cm is ______________________________.

3. The unit of area is ____________________.

   The unit of perimetre is ____________________.

4. The perimetre of a square is 72cm. The area of the square is ______________________________.

5. A rectangular playground is of 60 metres long and 45 metres broad. Another is a square playground of length 54 metres. Which is bigger? and by how much ?

   ____

   ____.

6. A hall 20m long and 15m broad is to be laid with bricks of length 20cm and breadth 10cm. The number of bricks required ______________________________.

Grade ________ Teacher's Signature ____________

Date ____________

Exercise 50

1. Answer the following.

   The length of the cuboid = _____

   The breadth of the cuboid = _____

   The height of the cuboid = _____

   The volume of the cuboid = ____________________

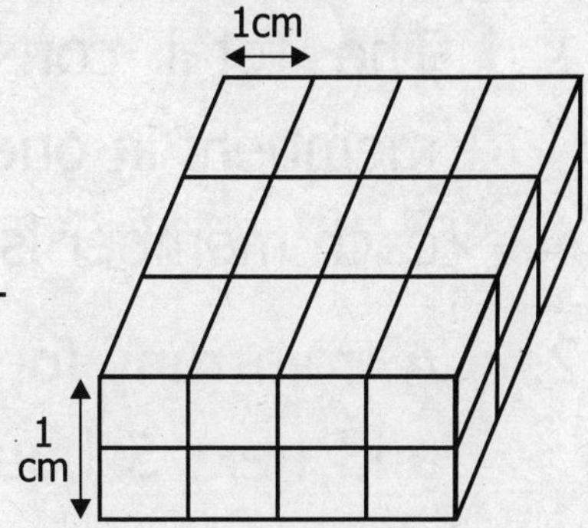

2. The difference between the volume of a cuboid and that of a cube is ____________________.

3. A water tank is 1m long, 0.5m broad and 0.4m high. The capacity of the tank in litres is ____________________.

4. The length, breadth and height of a room are 4.2m, 3.5m and 3m respectively. The volume of air in the room is ____________________.

5. If we put 10 small cubes of equal size together, the figure formed will be a cuboid. The volume of 1 small cube is 8 cu. cm, the volume of the cuboid is ____________________.

6. The outside dimensions of a wooden box are 1m x 0.9m x 0.6m. The inside dimensions are 0.8m x 0.6m x 0.5m. The volume of the wood used is ____________________.

Grade ________ Teacher's Signature ____________

Date ____________

Exercise 51

1. The total consumption of rice in a family of five members in one month is 15.5 kg. The consumption of each member is ______________________.

2. A train runs for 4 hours at a speed of 30 km per hour and next 5 hours at a speed of 42 km per hour. The average speed of the train is ____________________.

3. The average of first fifteen counting numbers is ____________________.

4. The average of first 6 multiples of 3 is ____________.

5. The following are the ages and heights of five students of a class.

	Age	Height
Sudesh	15 years 3 months	156 cm
Raman	16 years	160 cm
Avdesh	15 years 9 months	155 cm
Aditya	15 years 6 months	158 cm
Rohit	16 years 2 months	162 cm

The average age is ____________________

The average height is ____________________

Grade ________ Teacher's Signature ________________

Date ______________

Exercise 52

1. A train travels at a speed of 25 m per second. The speed in km per hour is ______________________.

2. A runner covered 2.5 km in 8 minutes. The speed in km per hour is ______________________.

3. A cyclist travels with a speed of 250 metres per minute. The time taken to cover a distance of 3000 metres is ______________________.

4. Compare 30 m per second and 72 km per hour. Which is more ? ______________________.

5. A train which runs at a speed of 65 km per hour takes 3 hours 15 minutes to travel from one station to another. The distance between two stations is ______________.

6. The speed of a scooter is 14.4 km per hour. The speed in m per second is ______________.

7. Ranjana ran 400 m in 8 minutes. Deepika ran 400 m in 6 minutes. Whose speed is more ? ______________.

   Express in km per hour ______________

Grade ________ Teacher's Signature ______________

Date ____________

Exercise 53

1. The simple interest on Rs 2200 for 5 years at 2½% per annum is ______________________________.

2. The amount is Rs 550 and principal is Rs 435. The interest is ______________________________.

3. Prepare a bill for the following items bought at Raman General Store.

   3 soaps at the rate of Rs. 7.50 each

   2 toothpaste at the rate of Rs 13.00 each

   5 noodle packets at the rate of Rs 7 each

   2 kg sugar at the rate of Rs 15 per kg

   If Sujan gave Rs 500 to the shopkeeper. The money he got in return is ______________________________.

4. A man borrowed Rs 800 at 5% per annum. At the end of 2½ years, he paid back an amount of Rs 450 and a watch for the balance amount. The cost of the watch is

   ____

   ______________________________.

Grade ________ Teacher's Signature ______________

Date ______________

Exercise 54

1. A petrol tank is 1m long, 0.5m broad and 0.4m high. The capacity of the tank in litres is ______________.

2. The area of a rectangle is 100 sq.cm. If the breadth of the rectangle is 8cm, the length is ______________.

3. A child runs at a speed of 10m per second. The time taken to cover a distance of 1 km is ______________.

4. The three sides of a triangle are 7.4cm, 5.1cm and 3.5cm long. Its perimeter is ______________.

5. The radius of a circle is 3cm. The approximate circumference is ______________.

6. The perimeter of a square is 46cm. The area of the square is ______________.

7. The perimeter of a triangle, whose sides 8cm, 5cm, 4cm in length is ______________.

8. The number of hours in 8100 seconds ______________ ______________.

Grade ________ Teacher's Signature ______________

Date ______________

Test Exercise 1

1. Which of te following is equivalent to 9%?

   a. 9   b. .009   c. .09   d. 0.9

2. The amount is Rs 630 and the interest is Rs 85. The principal is ______________________.

3. The cost of car was Rs 65000 in January and increased by 5% in February. The cost of the car in February was ______________________.

4. A man bought a TV set for Rs 10500 and sold it at a profit of Rs 350. If he had sold the TV set for Rs 15000, the extra profit he would have earned was ______________________.

5. An aeroplane starts from Delhi with a speed of 500 km per hour and reaches Amritsar airport in 40 minutes. The distance covered by the aeroplane ______________.

6. The value of

   a. 70% of 100 millilitres ______________________

   b. 1% of 100 rupees ______________________

   c. 90% of 500 marks ______________________

Grade __________ Teacher's Signature ______________________

Date ____________

Test Exercise 2

1. Write in numerals with commas according to the Indian System of numeration.
   a. Two crore nine lakh sixty-one thousand five hundred one. ____________
   b. Seventy lakh thirty-two thousand eighty-five. ____________
   c. Seventy two crore twenty lakh seventy-one thousand eight hundred ____________

2. Write the commas according to International System of numeration.
   a. 50832107 b. 629523 c. 21678954

3. Fill in the boxes with missing digits.

a.
$$\begin{array}{r} 3\ 5\ \square\ 4\ \square\ 7 \\ +\ \square\ 1\ 3\ \square\ 2\ \square \\ \hline 8\ \square\ 9\ 7\ 5\ 7 \\ \hline \end{array}$$

b.
$$\begin{array}{r} \square\ 6\ 4\ \square\ 8\ \square \\ -\ 1\ \square\ 4\ 1\ \square\ 0 \\ \hline \\ \hline \end{array}$$

4. Find the least number which after increased by 8 is exactly divisible by 18, 72 and 28. ____________

5. Fill in the boxes

a. $\frac{3}{5} + \frac{2}{15} = \frac{\square}{15}$ b. $\frac{8}{9} - \frac{\square}{12} = \frac{17}{\square}$

c. $\square \div 2\frac{3}{4} = \frac{12}{22}$ $35 \times \square = 39\frac{2}{3}$

Grade ________ Teacher's Signature ____________

Date ____________

6. Express as a percentage

a. $3\frac{1}{4}$ b. $\frac{5}{8}$ c. .5

7. Find the value of

a. 28% of 1020 b. 51% of 50 metres

8. Find

C.P. = Rs 849 SP = Rs 925 Profit = ________

C.P. = Rs 1089 Loss = ________ S.P. = ________

9. Convert

a. 645 mg = ________ dg b. 95 hm = ________ km

10. If 233.64 ÷ 76 = 3.14, find the quotient of

a. 2386.4 ÷ 7.6 b. 23.864 ÷ 7.6 c. 23864 ÷ 0.76

11. Name the angle

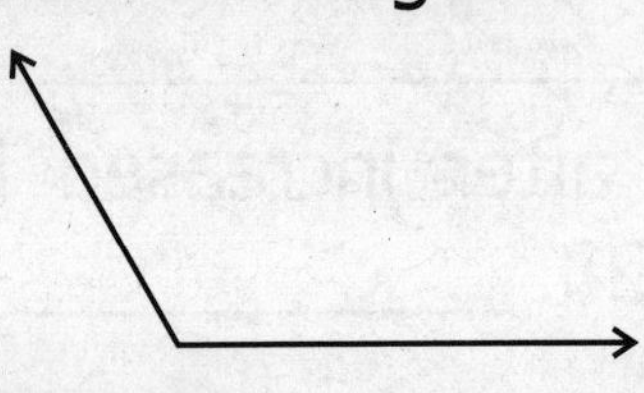

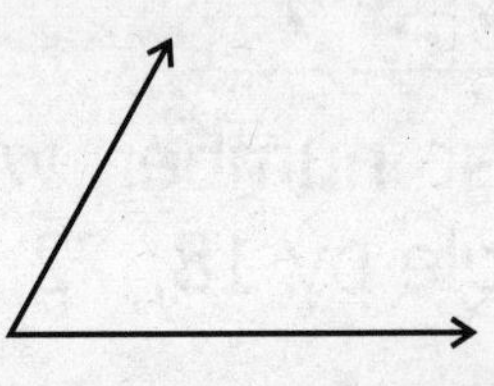

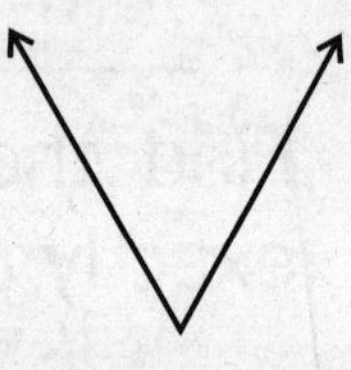

12. Simplify

a. $5\frac{1}{4} + 3\frac{1}{8} \div 1\frac{1}{4} - 1\frac{1}{4}$ b. 3.25 ÷ 0.25 + 8.5

13. Find the product

a. 10.001 x 10 b. 90.09 x 1000

Grade ________ Teacher's Signature ____________